FROM HEAD TO SOUL

A DAILY GUIDE TO PERSONAL STYLE AND INNER SELF CONFIDENCE

FOR WOMEN

By Joyce Knudsen, Ph.D.

Illustrations and design by Zora Bacon
Cover illustration by Michael Clark
Editing by A. Holland

SECOND EDITION

Library of Congress Control Number: 2001091175
ISBN# 0-9701744-0-3

Knudsen, Joyce, Ph.D.
From Head to Soul
http://www.imagemaker1.com

PRINTED IN THE UNITED STATES OF AMERICA BY
Morris Publishing • 3212 East Highway 30 • Kearney, NE 68847
1-800-650-7888

foreword

Every woman needs to be able to express her beauty. Sometimes we don't know how. Not every woman has an aunt or sister that has the gift of knowing just what looks good on her younger relative. I know I didn't. This book is an easily readable guide to help you recognize where you fit into a look and what will look best on you. Whether you are a mom, a teen, or someone going into the modeling business, this book can help you easily identify your best traits and accentuate them.

Do you ever wonder why the hairstyle that looks so great on her doesn't look good on you? Have you ever noticed that scarves look great on you? Have you never tried a scarf? This book will be your friend in telling you what will and won't work—in particular bathing suits. Who doesn't have a problem finding what works for them in a bathing suit? This book helped me determine my style for my form. And this book tells the truth—completely unbiased. Sometimes your best friend can't tell you that your outfit does not match because she does not want to hurt your feelings. Don't be afraid to look at yourself in the mirror and realize you may need a change.

Joyce Knudsen, Ph.D., knows what she's talking about. She's been an image counselor for years working with all walks of life. Let her help you. Joyce has been helping people discover who they are inside and out while exploring the keys that make people individuals. Every woman likes to feel beautiful. This book is a great tool for beauty. Use it!

Warmly, Heather Corwin
Actress of Stage and Screen

table of contents

acknowledgments

My deepest thanks and appreciation go to my wonderful husband Alan, and my two very special children, Kristen, and Justin, who together gave me the confidence, encouragement and support I needed to reach my goals. Without them, this book may not have been written.

Happiness cannot be traveled to, owned, worn or consumed. Happiness is the spiritual experience of living every minute with love, grace, and gratitude.
— Dennis Waitley

Only when you have attended to the smaller details of your appearance can you then go to town on the charm.
— F. Scott Fitzgerald

INTRODUCTION

You are very special, with unique characteristics that no one else possesses. The purpose of this "how to" book is to help you get to know who you are, to help you achieve "your individual new look" and to show you how you can become the best you can be. A positive attitude, an understanding of your unique characteristics, an appreciation of your own uniqueness and strong points are worthy goals to strive for. Each woman has her own individual beauty.

To be successful in life, we need to be emotionally well, physically fit, and spiritually sound. Whether you are a student, young adult, homemaker, secretary, teacher, business person, sales executive, trainee, clerk, or factory worker, this self-help book can be your daily guide to looking and feeling good about yourself.

It is a misconception to think that only people in certain positions or social situations need to look good. Many women walk around feeling unsure of themselves and probably feel that they are alone in these feelings. This simply is not true. We are all unsure of ourselves at one time or another depending on the circumstances. We are influenced by childhood experiences, peers, school, the environment, and the family. If we get positive acceptance from the things we do, we develop self confidence in these areas. If we get negative feedback from the things we do, we develop a lack of self confidence in these areas. If you acquire self acceptance within yourself, you will have the ability to accept others; if you feel self rejection within yourself, you will not be able to accept others. Self acceptance thus equals acceptance of others, whereas self rejection equals rejection of others.

Looking good on the outside is what makes people want to look inside to see what you are all about. The outside "shell" is the packaging for what lies within. The tongue can be untruthful, but the body acts with instinct. No matter how confident or sure of yourself you try to appear, you will always project how you feel about yourself on the inside. If you do not feel good about yourself physically or mentally, you will not make a good impression.

Self-image is an attitude, believing in yourself and in what you can do. You earn self confidence when you achieve. Here are some elements to consider for a strong development of self image.

1 • POSITIVE THINKING

You can control what you say and what you feel. A positive attitude will give you the best opportunity for positive results.

2 • STRONG SELF BELIEF

We are all unique and need to do what we feel is right, no matter how someone else feels about it. We have power over ourselves and do not need to let words or opinions of other people change the way we feel about ourselves. If you do what someone else wants you to do, you are not being yourself.

3 • FORTITUDE

Reach for what you want and get what you are after.

If you put yourself in a frame of mind that you have already made achievements, you are almost there. It's a self-fulfilling prophecy. Self confident people do positive things and earn self confidence in the process. They have a clear sense of who they are and what they want. They are achievers and are successful in life.

Looking your best through hairstyles, makeup and fashion is essential to building self confidence. Looking your best makes you feel good, and when you feel good you can accomplish more. However, much deeper than your outside appearance is your soul... the innermost part of you that must feel good. Feeling good from the inside will shine through on the outside. Your body will function at its best, and your skin will glow. Most of all, you will experience the wonderful feeling of being whole, from the inside out.

Within you right now is the power to do things you never dreamed possible. This power becomes available to you just as soon as you can change your beliefs.
— *Maxwell Maltz*

You cannot always control circumstances but you can control your own thoughts.
— *Charles Pepplestown*

The future belongs to those who believe in the beauty of their dreams.
— *Eleanor Roosevelt*

WHAT READERS SAY

Very well-written, informative, and easy to follow. After reading this book, you will be the best you can be without the high cost and time of attending an etiquette or modeling school.

— Yvonne Marie Felster
Actress/Model

"BRAVO!"... Finally, a step-by-step book for all ages on how to improve outer AND inner body appearance and gain self confidence for a lifetime of success!

— Kathy Pooles
Acting/Modeling Instructor

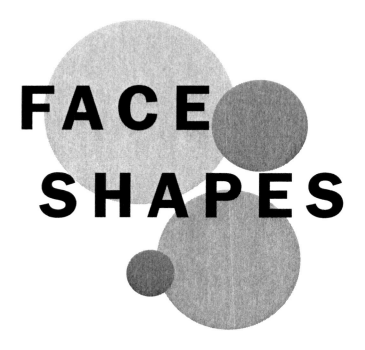

It is not easy to find happiness in ourselves and it is impossible to find it elsewhere.

— Agnes Reppliere

four basic face shapes

There is no such thing as an ugly woman. There are only the ones who do not know how to make themselves attractive.

– *Christian Dior*

To work with and benefit from this book, the first thing necessary to determine is your facial shape. To determine your facial shape, begin by pulling all of your hair away from your forehead and around your face. Look into a mirror and determine which illustration resembles your facial shape. Imagine an outline of your face. Does your face have the most fullness at the forehead area? If so, you have a heart or triangular shaped face. Does your face have a squared-off appearance where the length and width of the face appear about the same? If so, you have a square facial shape. If your face appears more rounded, you have a round facial shape. If your face appears the widest in the cheek area and tapers off toward the chin area, you have an oval shaped face.

The goal in determining facial shape is to balance the look... your look... the one that is best for you! The ideal facial shape is the oval which can adapt to any hat or hairstyle. The round, square, and heart facial shapes can "appear" to be oval by balancing the face properly.

To follow, there will be a guide to choosing hairstyles for your particular facial shape. On the round, square, and heart shaped drawings, you will see an incorrect and then a correct hairstyle. Note that the oval shaped face can wear any hairstyle.

Once you have determined your facial shape, you are on your way to discovering the secret to becoming the very best you can be.

round

The length and width of your face
are the same. When hair is pulled back
away from the face, your face appears
to be round.

square

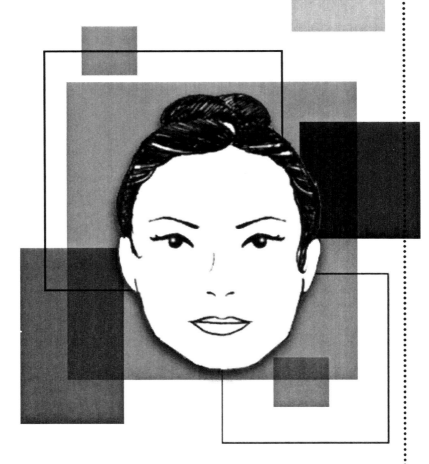

The length and width are about the same, but the face is more squared-off. A variation of this face shape is the rectangle, which is slightly longer from top to bottom.

oval

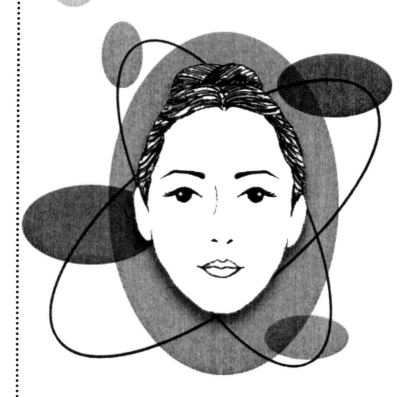

The widest part is in the area of the cheekbone. This face shape tapers off from the cheekbone to the chin and can be considered "egg-shaped". A variation is the oblong face, which is slightly longer from the chin to the forehead.

heart

The widest part of your face is in the forehead, and the chin curves inward. The heart shaped face is also known as the triangular shaped face.

The kind of beauty I want most is the hard-to-get kind that comes from within—strength, courage, dignity.

— *Ruby Dee*

hairstyles

A crown makes a queen; a hairstyle makes a woman.

– *Kristen Knudsen*

Hairstyles change constantly. One season short hair is "in," the next season, long hair is "in." The key to your best look is to find the hairstyle that is right for your face judged according to your jawline and facial structure. You'll know that you have the "right" hairstyle when it feels comfortable, looks good, and works well with your facial shape.

ROUND FACIAL SHAPE

A round facial shape has full cheeks and chin with a rounded forehead. This facial shape requires a shorter cut put forward onto the face for texture and volume (see illustration). This moves the eye away from the roundness and adds interest. Wearing a medium length hairstyle with height on top, avoiding chin length and blunt bangs, and putting your part off-center also work well for this facial shape. A round face needs height. Bring hair onto cheeks and remember to keep to one side.

ROUND

incorrect

ROUND

correct

SQUARE FACIAL SHAPE

A square or rectangle facial shape has wide cheekbones, and a squared forehead and jaw. These facial shapes have a straight hairline. A shorter cut put forward onto the face takes the eye away from the squareness and adds interest. A short or medium length cut with soft height on top is best for this facial shape. A square face needs more height than the rectangular face, but otherwise the same rules apply. Choose a style that hugs the jawline, but avoid bangs.

SQUARE

incorrect

SQUARE

correct

HEART FACIAL SHAPE

A heart facial shape is wide at the forehead and narrow in the chin area. A shoulder length hairstyle, parted to one side, will balance this facial shape. This shape needs volume and fullness at the middle and bottom of the style, such as a full flip. Variations of the heart face shape are the inverted triangle or pear shape, where the forehead is more narrow than the chin area. In this case you want to bring out the fullness at the forehead to balance out this shape, which can be achieved through the use of bangs. Remember, you want to add fullness where you are lacking it, and take away fullness where you have too much.

HEART
incorrect

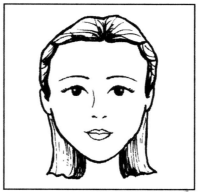

HEART
correct

OVAL FACIAL SHAPE

Remember, what you want to accomplish is a style that is right for you. It is absolutely necessary to choose a hairstyle that will make you look your best. An oval face can wear any style; however, if you tend to be more oblong, you will want to balance out this shape by keeping the hairstyle from making your face appear too long. Avoid too much height at the top and extremely long lengths.

OVAL
short hair

OVAL
long hair

CHOOSING THE RIGHT HAIRSTYLE FOR YOU

• Begin by looking through fashion magazines and cutting out pictures of styles that you like, and that seem to be on a model with a similar face shape to yours.

• Determine the time you will need to maintain the style that you are considering.

• Arrange for a few consultations with stylists that are either recommended to you or that you know do styles similar to the ones you have chosen. If a stylist is not willing to give you a consultation, choose another stylist. You will want to choose someone who is willing to spend time with you and develop you as his or her customer.

• Be sure to maintain your new look with regular trims and conditioning treatments.

The style you choose should emphasize your best features and complement the shape and size of your face. It must be comfortable and easy to work with, so that maintaining your new style will not be difficult.

It's no exaggeration to say that a strong positive self-image is the best possible preparation for success in life.

— Dr. Joyce Brothers

The body is a test tube. You have to put in exactly the right ingredients to get the best reaction out of it.

– Jack Youngblood

nutrition and your health

A WORD ABOUT NUTRITION

Destiny shapes our ends, but calorie intake is what shapes our middles.
— Author Unknown

While it is important to choose the right hairstyle and wear makeup, in order to give your body a head to soul boost, there is no better beauty basic than to provide a plan for what you eat. A well balanced diet puts shine in your hair, sparkle in your eyes, and a glow to your skin. You will look better, and you will feel better about yourself.

Combine proper nutrition with exercise. Consult your physician first to see if you can put yourself on an exercise program for at least 45 minutes, 3 times a week. According to the book *Fit For Life* by Harvey and Marilyn Diamond, "for the body cycles to function effectively, it is imperative to integrate the outlined principles of good eating habits with a well balanced exercise program." Choose swimming, tennis, jumping rope, bike riding, walking, jogging or aerobic classes, but do something! It will enhance your beauty and make you feel great!

JUST RIGHT?

- Exercise 30 minutes at least three times a week.
- Check weight and measurements often to assure control.
- Eat three balanced meals a day.
- Drink 6-8 glasses of water a day.

OVERWEIGHT?

- Exercise 30 minutes each day.
- Set a goal to lose 2-3 pounds a week.
- Eat three balanced meals a day. Cut food intake in half.
- Drink 6-8 glasses of water a day.
- Keep busy.
- Stop eating before you are full.
- Chew your food thoroughly and eat slowly.
- Do not use much salt in foods. It slows down weight loss.
- Consult your physician.

UNDERWEIGHT?

- Exercise leisurely.
- Eat three balanced meals a day with mid-morning and mid-afternoon snacks.
- Eat more slowly and chew your food thoroughly.
- Rest before and after meals to allow for easier digestion.
- Keep warm on cold and windy days.
- Have a malt or protein shake daily.
- Add jam to bread and butter; butter to vegetables; rich dressing to your salads; gravy and cream sauces to meats and vegetables.
- Don't be discouraged. Weight gaining is slower than losing.
- Learn to slow down. Rushing keeps weight down.
- Consult your physician.

THE FOOD PYRAMID

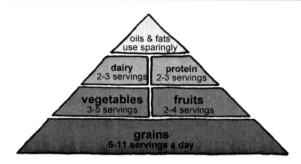

The United States Department of Agriculture has seen the benefits of using the Food Pyramid. Listed in the Journal of The American Medical Association, there was a study done over a twelve year period with 42,000 U.S. women that showed that those whose diets most resembled the pyramid had the lowest risk of dying from any cause. The statistics discovered were a 40% lower cancer risk, a 33% lower heart disease risk and a 42% lower stroke risk.

The pyramid gives you a diet low in fat and sugar and gives you complex carbohydrates, protein, fiber, vitamins, and minerals.

Here are suggested servings for each category:
• Grains: 1/4 cup cooked rice or pasta or one slice of bread.
• Produce: one cup of raw vegetables (1/4 cup if cooked) or fruit.
• Protein: 3 to 4 ounces of meat, chicken or fish, 1.5 cooked beans, or 3 eggs.
• Dairy - one cup yogurt or milk.

For additional information, go to www.usda.gov.cnpp. If you log on to this site, the government will tell you how your pyramid reads. If you enter everything you eat for one day, you will get a result of how you are doing compared with the standard.

Eating healthy and exercising three times a day for twenty minutes, or enough time to work up a sweat, will help you feel better and live longer.

skin care

Your skin is the largest organ in the body and is 90% water. The other components that make up skin are collagen and protein.

Skin is very important. It eliminates waste and helps keep the body temperature. To properly take care of our skin, we must be on a daily skin care program that consists of cleansing, toning, and moisturizing.

DAILY CLEANSING ROUTINE

• CLEANSING
Cleansing removes dirt, pollution and dead surface cells.

• TONING
Toning stimulates and tightens pores.

• MOISTURIZING
Moisturizing returns moisture removed in the first two processes, and seals in the skin's natural moisture. Be sure your hands and your towel are clean. Pull your hair away from your face. Apply cold cream, cleansing cream, or liquid makeup remover carefully to your face. Never rub, always pat the skin. Remove makeup from your eye area and lips first. You do not want to spread the makeup all over your face. With a slightly fingertips, apply cleanser to your cheeks, nose, forehead and chin with both upward and downward strokes to remove all the dirt from your face. Rinse thoroughly and pat dry with a towel. Put on a toner to balance out your skin's pH. Protect your clean face with a moisturizer. Your skin will only absorb the moisturizer it needs, so start with a light amount and you will be able to tell if you need more in certain areas. Remember the neck area. Be sure to choose skin products that will benefit your skin type. To determine skin type, try the tissue test on the next page.

TISSUE TEST

In the morning when your face is free of any makeup, tear off small pieces of tissue and apply them to various areas of your face. Hold there about 20 seconds to allow the skin oils to emerge. Be sure to do this on the nose, cheeks and chin. Oily skin will turn the tissue completely translucent, dry skin will not show a change, and combination skin will turn some areas oily while leaving other areas dry.

When you have the result of your skin type, you will know what products to look for. If you have combination skin, you will need products for oily skin for oily areas, and products for dry skin for your dry areas.

Repeat this test to keep a record of complexion changes, as skin is influenced by biological factors such as age and environment. The cleansing process keeps our skin at a healthy pH and in balance. The enemies of skin are the sun's ultraviolet rays, pollution, and cigarettes. Since these enemies are part of society, we must be aware that our skin will need extra attention.

It is not necessary to have a lot of skin care products. Besides a cleanser, toner and moisturizer, all that is needed is a facial mask and a facial scrub once a week to remove excess oils and slough off dead skin cells. With these tips, you will bring your skin to a healthy glow.

Once a week, you can deep cleanse your face with a refreshing herbal steam. Boil a large pot of water. Add several chamomile tea bags and let soak for about ten minutes. Pour the water into your sink and with a towel draped over your head, close your eyes and let the steam open your pores for about ten minutes. Rinse with cold water and pat your face dry. This is great for cleaning up whiteheads, blackheads, and pimples.

SKIN COMPOSITION

Skin is composed of:

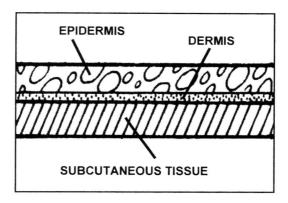

EPIDERMIS

The top layer is made of keratinized protein which protects the skin from dryness and bacteria. The lower layers of the epidermis are the new cell manufacturing sites. As cells grow, they push toward the surface of the skin. They have completed their cycle by the time they reach the top of the skin. They have become dead protein. These need to be removed by thorough cleansing.

DERMIS

The dermis lies beneath the epidermis and is where the trouble begins. The dermis forms the support system of the skin. This layer contains oil, sweat glands, hair follicles, blood vessels and fat glands. The dermis is also where collagen is found—a type of support for the face.

TYPES OF SKIN

DRY SKIN

Dry skin has a tendency to flake and chap. It is sensitive to the weather elements, such as cold and dry air, wind and sun. This type of skin rarely has breakouts since the pores are usually small. This type of skin requires rich oils to keep it smooth. Remove makeup with a rich makeup remover high in emollients. Take makeup off with something other than tissue. Cotton squares work beautifully. Choose a natural glycerine (soapless) cleanser, such as French-milled soap. Rinse thoroughly. Follow with skin toner that does not contain any alcohol, and complete with moisturizing lotion to help keep the natural oils in the skin.

OILY SKIN

Oily skin keeps your skin looking young, but it needs special attention. It is a misconception that putting a strong astringent on this skin type will stop the problem of oily skin. If the epidermis becomes too dry, then the dermis underneath (where most of the skin problems occur) may actually cause the skin to become oilier. It is almost like putting the dermis into shock. It is fine to use an astringent with a low alcohol content to combat an oil problem. This type of skin would benefit from mild facial soaps, oatmeal, fruit or herbal soaps, gel cleansers, oil-free cleansing lotions, astringents or toner afterwards. To moisturize, use an oil-free, water-based moisturizer only when needed in areas that need moisturizing. Once a week, use an oil-absorbing mud or clay mask, and a mild facial scrub.

COMBINATION SKIN

Combinations skin is oily down the T-zone- your forehead, nose and chin- and dry around the eye and cheek area. To cleanse your face, use a glycerin or castile soap, or nongreasy lotion or cream cleansers. You can use an astringent with a low alcohol content on the oily areas and a toner on the dry areas. To moisturize, use emollient or replenishing creams on the dry areas, and water-based lotions or oil-free moisturizers on the oily areas. To condition, use an astringent-like mask such as lemon or pear, or a slightly moisturizing yogurt mask.

SENSITIVE SKIN

Sensitive skin requires mild unscented soaps, baby soap or hypoallergenic cleansers. Avoid natural ingredients like fruits or vegetables which have a tendency to cause allergic reactions. To moisturize, use a lanolin-free lotion, unscented cream, or hypoallergenic moisturizer. To condition once a week, use soothing cream masks and mild sloughing masks for gentle exfoliation.

BREAKOUTS

Breakouts require special attention with sulfur soaps, oil-absorbing soap, mild abrasive oatmeal, seaweed or brown sugar soaps, medicated acne soaps, or medicated cleansing pads. To moisturize, use water-based, oil-free moisturizer where needed. To condition breakout-prone skin once a week, use a clay or mud mask, oil-free mask, light peeling mask or, mild exfoliating treatment (use only when the skin is not broken out!), and avoid harsh facial scrubs.

makeup

To determine your skin tone, try this test:
1. Put a tan or beige-toned foundation on your cheek.
2. Put a pink-toned foundation on the opposite cheek.
3. Determine which foundation blends in best.

TYPES OF SKIN TONES

The best way to determine your skin tone is to become familiar with what looks best on your skin. Skin either has a warm or cool tone, or sometimes a combination of warm and cool. If you take foundation in both a beige and a pink tone, you can use the following experiment.

If your skin has a warm tone, the beige foundation will blend in and the pink-based foundation will appear to stay on top of your skin. If your skin has a cool tone, the opposite will occur. The pink-based foundation will blend and the beige will appear to stay on the surface of the skin. This is because we are born with skin undertones that never change. With this knowledge, you will be able to purchase makeup and clothing that will be complementary to your particular skin tone.

Apply all foundation lightly with a water-softened foam rubber wedge, or makeup sponge. There should be no indication of where foundation starts and stops. It is most important to blend thoroughly. If you choose not to wear foundation, a light dusting of powder will give you a polished, natural look.

HIGHLIGHT AND SHADOW AREAS

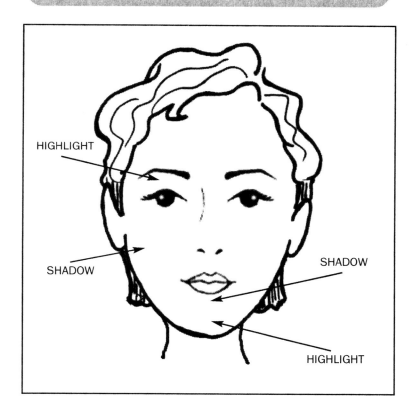

HIGHLIGHT

SHADOW

SHADOW

HIGHLIGHT

HIGHLIGHT	VERSUS	SHADOW
Areas that are too narrow, deep-set eyes, under lower lip and chin if necessary.		Areas that are too wide, protruding orbital bone, nose, jaw and chin if necessary.

- LIGHT REVEALS: Where you want to bring out...
- DARK CONCEALS: Where you want to take away...

EYEBROW GUIDE

Your eyebrows are very important because they frame your eyes and add expression to your face!

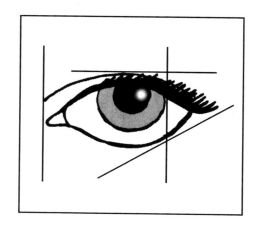

SHAPING YOUR BROWS

Using the above diagram as a guide, follow these directions to properly shape and groom your eyebrows:

Line up a pencil against your nostril and over the tear duct of your eye. The pencil should intersect your brow line. If it does not, then mark with a colored pencil (such as an eyeliner pencil) where your eyebrow should begin. Hold the pencil on the diagonal so it touches the outer edge of your nostril, and your outer eye corner. Extend the diagonal line to the outer edge of your brow and make sure that it is aligned. Mark again, where your brow should end. Feel your browbone with your fingers. The arch should follow its contours.

When tweezing, hold the skin taut between the thumb and forefinger. Using the marks you made as a guide, pluck the excess hairs from the underside of your brows, tweezing them one at a time in the direction of hair growth, which is upward and outward. To groom brows, apply gel to your brow brush and brush up and out. Eyebrows should be groomed on a weekly basis. Eyebrows should be the same color or lighter than your hair so that they do not overpower your face.

EYE CHART

SMALL EYES

Small eyes need a pale shade over entire lid and browbone and a darker color in the crease. Apply liner along upper lashes and along the lower outside corners of your eyes.

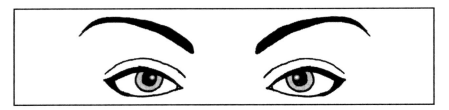

FULL EYES

Full eyes have too much lid visible in comparison to the above-eye crease area. You would put lighter shadow on the upper lid, stopping before the eye-crease and put a deeper shadow where the lighter shadow ends, extending up into crease and blend. To complete, line the eye top and bottom.

ALMOND EYES

Almond eyes have the appearance of the outer corners of eyes being lower than the inner corners. Lighter shadow should go on the upper lid and deeper shadow should go in the crease, going in and out from the center of eye to the outer corner. Put a deeper shadow under the lower lashes, from the outer corner to the center and line the upper lid all the way across the eye, broadening at the outer third. Line the outer third of the lower lid around at corner.

NARROW LIDS

Narrow lids have very little upper lid when the eyes are open. Apply lighter shadow across the lid and deeper shadow in the crease and above. Line the outer third of upper and lower lids close to the lashes. Blend.

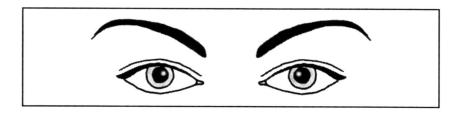

CLOSE SET EYES

Close set eyes have less than the size of one eye between the inner corners of the eyes. You would put lighter shadow from the inner corner up to the brow and across the lid, and deeper shadow across the crease, extending up and out beyond the outer corner just a little. Only line the outer two thirds of the upper lid and the outer third of the lower lid and blend well. This will make the eyes appear to be further apart.

WIDE SET EYES

Wide set eyes have more than one eye width between the inner corners of the eyes. Apply lighter shadow on the lid and deeper shadow from the crease to below the brow on inner half of eye and from a little above the crease on the outer half. Be careful not to extend beyond the outer corner as these eyes want to appear closer together. Line the upper lid and broaden the line at the inner third. Line the lower lid on only the outer third of the eye and blend.

DEEP SET EYES

Deep set eyes have an overly-prominent browbone and the eyes look as though they are recessed or closed in. Apply lighter shadow on the upper lid to about a quarter of the way before the outer corner. Apply a deeper shadow on the outer edge of the lid up to browbone and blend. Line only the outer third of the lower lid and blend.

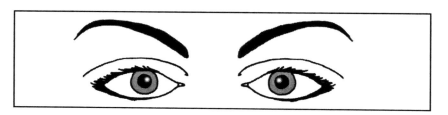

EYESHADOWS

Eyeshadow can be bought as a cream, stick, liquid, crayon, powder, or pressed cake. The pressed cake type can be applied wet or dry. It comes with a sponge tip applicator. Use the round end for application and the pointed end to smudge under the eye for blending. Eye crayons are easy to apply.

Be sure to choose eyeshadows in neutral tones that complement your skin tone. Do not match your eyeshadow to your eye color. Always blend in by smudging. You cannot make a mistake by putting on too much if you are blending well. Use an eyeshadow brush, using short vertical strokes and blending as you work on the eye area.

• Cream Shadows: best for dry skin and are easy to apply.

• Powder Shadows: best for oily skin types, as they hold in oils. These should be applied with a brush.

• Pencil/Crayon Shadows: provide soft color, more defined lines, and more control. They are easy to apply, once you learn how, and stay on longer.

TYPES OF MAKEUP

Now that the eyes are ready, concealer and foundation can be applied. The reason we apply the eye makeup first is so that the eyes do not run onto the foundation creating smudges.

CONCEALER

Concealer is used to hide imperfections like skin discolorations or dark circles under the eyes. It should be applied under your foundation and then over, blending well. Do not carry the concealer over on to your cheeks. It need only be directly under your eyes to bring them out.

CONTOUR

Contour can be used at this time, if necessary. This can be used in the form of a darker foundation, or powder, and the purpose is to take away from a particular area.

FOUNDATION

Foundation then will give an even tone and polish to your skin in addition to covering blemishes and protecting the skin from the elements in the environment such as wind, cold, sun and pollution. Choose your foundation to match your skin tone.

BLUSH

Blush then is used to emphasize the cheekbones and to soften harsh natural lines. The shade of your blush is determined by your skin tone, not by the color of your clothes. The purpose of blush is to brighten your skin and highlight your bone structure. Everyone has a different facial shape; therefore, everyone should not wear blush the same way.

POWDER

Powder is used to hold foundation, concealer, contour and blush in place. Put on with a sponge or brush to set your makeup.

LIPSTICK

Lipstick defines and outlines the lips and adds color to the face.

WATER

Water in a spray bottle will help to give your face a natural glow and makes your makeup look so natural that it will appear as if you aren't wearing any!

ENHANCING CHEEKBONES

To enhance high cheekbones, apply a cream blush from just outside the apple of your cheek, along the cheekbone out to the hairline. Always blend well. If you need to enhance your cheekbones, darker foundation or contour powder will give you a more defined cheekbone if you apply along the base of the bone. Put a lighter shade of foundation over the top and blend well. Set with translucent powder. Work lightly with your blush brush and build up layers rather than putting blush on too dark.

To apply blush, dip into powder and dab on your hand to remove excess. Lightly brush the color on cheekbones from ear to nose and slowly build up layers rather than putting blush on all at once.

After applying blush, lightly dust your face with powder to tone down and set all makeup. If you prefer cream, liquid or gel blush, these should be applied with a dampened sponge, or fingertips, and blended well. You want to avoid having two red circles on your cheeks!!

ROUND FACE

A round face is accented by placing blush in the center of cheeks directly below the pupil of the eye and blending down toward the mouth.

SQUARE FACE

A square face is accented by applying blush in a diagonal path ending parallel to your brow.

HEART FACE

A heart face is accented by placing the blush on the center of the cheekbone in line below the end of the eye and straight up.

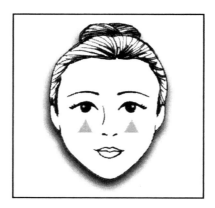

OVAL FACE

An oval face is accented by applying blush high on the cheekbones directly beneath the eye, blended upward and outward to the hairline.

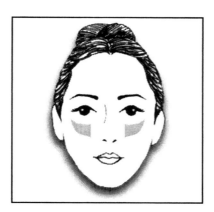

LIPS

Lip color should brighten your face. You must stay within your skin tone when choosing a lip color. If you wear a color that is too bright or too light for your skin tone, you will give your lips too much attention.

Use the following guidelines to bring your lips into perfect proportion:

THIN LIPS

First apply foundation over entire lip area. Then outline lips wih pencil just outside of natural lipline. Fill with lip color.

FULL LIPS

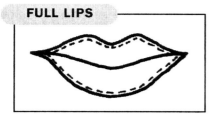

Apply foundation over lips. Pencil lips just inside natural lipline. Apply lip color within this line only.

FLAT LIPS

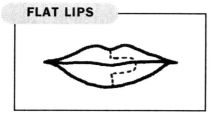

Give flat lips a plumper look by applying color over entire lips except at very center. Fill in center space with a lighter, shimmery color. Aim for a subtle look; don't make the line between the two colors obvious.

CRINKLY LIPS

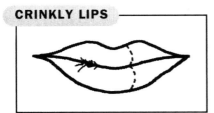

To give these lips shine, apply color, then apply lots of gloss on top. Some vaseline applied at night will help the dryness problem.

DROOPY LIPS

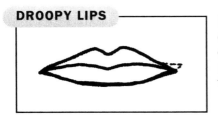

Lift them at the corners by first covering lip corners with a concealer stick. Blend. Using lip pencil, extend lip corner up, and fill with color.

UNEVEN LIPS

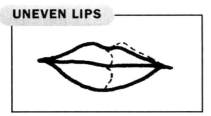

Balance uneven lips or soften a too-sharp bow at center by outlining the desired shape with a lip pencil. Fill in with color in shade close to pencil color.

eyewear

....

Stop hiding behind those frames—have glass class! Choose a face-flattering frame in a color that goes with your skin tone and let your eyes shine through.

Choose a square or geometrical frame shape.

To soften the angles of your face,
choose rounded or aviator shapes.

HEART FACE

Choose a frame that will narrow the width
of the top portion of your face,
such as a round or oval frame.

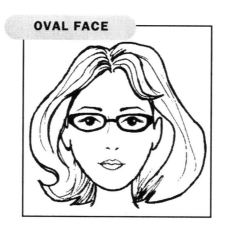

OVAL FACE

An oval face can wear any type of frame, but if your face tends to be
more heart shaped, avoid thickness and fullness across the top. You
need to balance the width of your forehead and chin.

Choosing glasses is a matter of balance. Where you are wide, you
want to take away. Where you are narrow, you want to bring out.
Choose a glass frame that is the most flattering to your facial shape.

A curved line is the loveliest distance between two points.

— *Mae West*

style

It would be nice if we were all built in perfect proportion. In order for us to look and feel our best, we must strive for the proper balance for our particular figure type.

Fashion fades, style is eternal.

— *Yves St. Laurent*

UNDERSTANDING YOUR FIGURE

What counts most for a woman is to be perfectly comfortable with herself. It is important that the clothes we choose fit our individual body type.

If you want to look your best in clothes, know your body and proportion. Use camouflage and contour to compensate for figure faults. Using the perfect figure model, note the following facts:

- Distance from hipbone to top of head equals distance from hipbone to feet
- Knees equally divide the lower half of your body
- Bust and hip measurement are the same with 10 inches less for waist
- Elbows meet waistline
- Fingertips touch mid-thigh
- Width across shoulders equals distance from neck to waist
- Well-formed shoulders mark a T
- Always maintain good posture

the illusion of dressing

Illusion is the secret of beauty.

– George Masters

Fashion is architecture unknown. It is a matter of proportions.

– Coco Chanel

The principals of line, balance and proportion form an illusion to the eye, and in dressing, this can work to your advantage.

• LINE plays an important part in dressing. The eyes "see" where clothing starts and stops and focus in these areas. Most outfits have lines that are vertical, horizontal, or diagonal. The eye will go toward the dominant line because it will stand out. For example, if you are wearing an outfit that has vertical lines, you will appear taller.

• PROPORTION has nothing to do with our height. What is important in proportion is to understand how we can look balanced. If you are short-waisted with long legs, you will not look the same as a person who is long-waisted and has short legs. We must learn to dress for our particular figure type.

Play up your favorite areas and downplay your not so good ones. Some lines give the illusion of height, some add weight, accent a certain body area, cut off a certain body area, add softness, or interest, make the body look thinner of heavier, or shorten your figure.

TO ENLARGE A PARTICULAR AREA, USE THE FOLLOWING:
• big prints, plaids or checks
• bright and light colors
• horizontal lines
• contrasting colors
• thick, rough textures
• shiny textures

TO DIMINISH A PARTICULAR AREA, USE THE FOLLOWING:
• small prints and checks
• dark colors
• vertical lines
• solid colors
• smooth fabrics
• matte finish

REMEMBER: light reveals.... dark conceals!

proportion guidelines

NECKLINES

ROUND

INCORRECT   CORRECT

- Round face shapes should wear V-necklines and drop earrings

SQUARE

INCORRECT   CORRECT

- Square face shapes should wear scoop or V-necklines.

HEART

INCORRECT   CORRECT

- Heart face shapes should wear turtlenecks, chokers, scarves and cluster earrings.

OVAL

INCORRECT   CORRECT

- Oval face shapes should wear turtlenecks, and thin or dangling earrings.

BUSTLINE

• LARGE: choose wide armholes and sleeves and some fullness on the top to avoid clinging at the bustline.

• FLAT: Use padded bras, pockets, ruffles, and lace across the bustline.

HIPS

• WIDE: choose diagonal pockets, lighter colors above the waistline, accented shoulders, and bloused effects above the waist.

BUTTOCKS

• LARGE: loosely fitted garments at the small of the back, and overblouses will make the buttocks appear smaller.

LEGS

• HEAVY: seamed, dark-colored hosiery works well.

• THIN: seamless, light-colored hosiery works well.

ARMS

• LARGE AND BROAD: choose wide rings with high dome or elongated ornaments, and larger bracelets.

• SLIM AND SMALL: small cluster rings and narrow bracelets work well.

All clothing is designed with a combination of straight, vertical, diagonal, and horizontal lines. Lines in clothing give interest to the piece and make the patterns more appealing to wear. Your body's proportions will be the determining factor in what type of lines are right for you.

SOME COMMON PROBLEMS

- small shoulders
- wide shoulders
- small bustline
- large bustline
- small waist
- large waist
- excessive abdomen or derriere

The rule of thumb is to wear vertical lines where you want to lengthen and elongate, such as with wide shoulders, large bustline, and large waist, and to wear horizontal lines where you want to widen or add to, such as with small shoulders, small bustline, and small waist. You would wear vertical lines below the waist with an excessive abdomen or derriere.

Wherever we are small, we want to bring out, and by using the horizontal line, we are accomplishing this. Wherever we are large, we want to take away, and we accomplish this by wearing the vertical line. The line will bring the eye to a more appealing place and balance out your figure.

You can determine where your lines should fall by looking in a full length mirror. You will begin to notice where you want to "reveal" and where you want to "conceal," as with makeup. Make the decision to use a vertical line where you want to take away. The result: a beautiful, balanced body.

What's in a name? A 35% markup.

– *Vince Thurston*

figure types

The only way to know what type of clothes look good on you is for you to know your body type. Wearing the proper clothes proportionately right for you can and does make a difference. Just because a particular style is "in" does not mean this style is right for you.

TO DETERMINE YOUR BODY TYPE

1. Stand in front of a full-length mirror.
2. Analyze yourself. Which body type do you think you are?

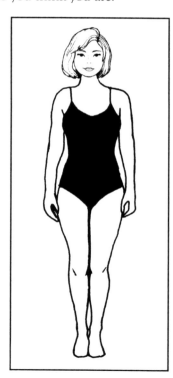

• If your shoulders and bust are about the same size and you curve in at the waist, you have an hourglass figure.

• If your shoulders, waist and hips are about the same size, you have a straight figure.

• If your hips and thighs are wider than your shoulders, you have a triangular figure.

• If your shoulders are wider than your hips and thighs, you have an inverted triangular figure.

• Re-evaluate yourself yearly. Our bodies change periodically.

Keep your body in balance by knowing your figure type!

hourglass

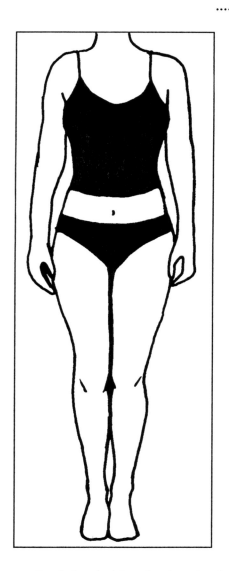

This is the easiest figure to work with. You can wear dramatic clothing and also body-conscious styles. You can wear fitted tops and fitted bottoms with emphasis on your small waist.

• Call attention to waist and midriff with belts.

• De-emphasize bust with non-clingy tops.

• Emphasize curve of hip with two-piece jersey dresses or fitted pants.

• Balance between top and bottom.

Look for clothing that has simple lines and follows the soft curves of your hourglass figure.

straight

When you have this figure type, you are straight all the way from your shoulders to your feet. There is no defined waistline, and both the top and bottom of the body are of equal width. You can wear anything an hourglass type can wear, but you have to be conscious about creating a waistline to balance out your figure.

• Elongate by using vertical lines, such as longer dresses, v-necks, and long jewelry.

• De-emphasize a heavy back by wearing loose sweaters and tops.

• Draw eyes to the middle and away from shoulders and hips.

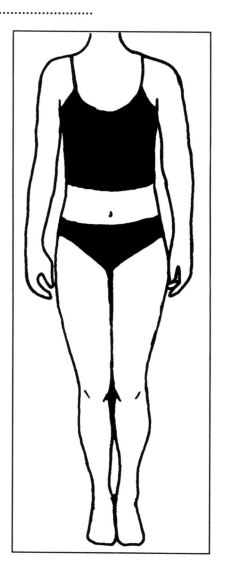

Look for clothing that creates the illusion of a smaller waist.

triangle

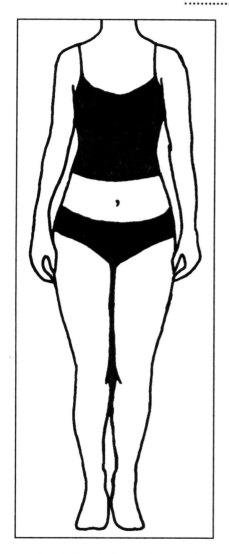

This figure type has sloping shoulders, a small bustline, and an ample hip and thigh area. This type needs width at the top of the body. Horizontal lines answer this need, as well as lighter colors on top, and darker colors on bottom.

• Emphasize the midriff and waist with belts.

• Broaden the upper torso with full sleeves and detailing.

• De-emphasize hips and thighs with dark bottoms and a-line skirts.

• Give the illusion of top and bottom balance with light tops and dark bottoms.

• De-emphasize derriere with panty girdles and shaping hosiery.

Look for clothing that emphasizes the waist, broadens shoulder line and softly skirts over hip and thigh area.

inverted triangle

This figure type has wide shoulders and large upper area, and is smaller in the lower part of the body. The opposite rules apply for this type than for the triangle figure type.

- Emphasize bottom by wearing prints or brights.

- De-emphasize top by choosing vertical lines and dark colors

- Give illusion of balance with dark colors on top and lighter colors on bottom.

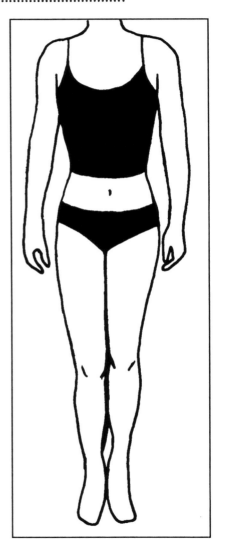

Look for clothing that empahsizes the lower part of the body and de-emphasizes the top.

petites

According to the National Center of Health Statistics, 55% of the adult population in the United States is 5'4" and under. This is approximately 24 million people. A woman is petite if she is 4'8" to 5'4" and weighs 85-126 pounds. Being petite has generally to do with height, not with size. A woman can be 5'1" and wear a large size. People who fall into the petite category should buy their clothing to fit their special figure type.

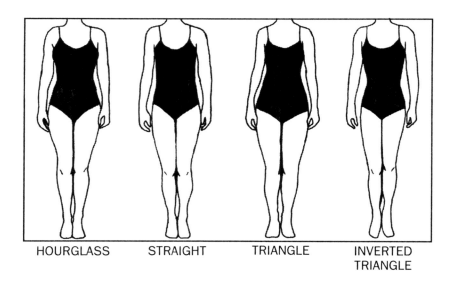

HOURGLASS   STRAIGHT   TRIANGLE   INVERTED TRIANGLE

It is important for this figure type to avoid bulk, stay in the same color family, use narrower belts, smaller accessories, vertical striping in their clothing, shorter jackets, lace or ruffles on top, and unconstructed, straight-fitting jackets. Petite skirts should have some gathers or shirring in front, and be fitted. Large, oversized collars would be too much for this small frame. Be sure shoulders fit at the shoulder line. For suits, you can use shoulder pads to add bulk to your frame. The shoulder pad you choose should be in balance with your body size. For example, a large petite would choose a smaller shoulder pad. Sleeves should be fitted and not too full.

Tapered pants will slenderize and lengthen. If you are short waisted with short legs, avoid pants with a wide waistband. Capitalize on what will look great: pants that flatter your legs and make you look taller. If you are long waisted and have short legs, it is most important that your pants should fit properly and be tapered. A high or wide waistband will lengthen your legs.

If your stomach area is rounded, never, never, never wear tight pants. Elastic waistbands and pleated-front pants are best.

If you are heavy in the hip area and have short legs, pants should never be tight fitting in these areas. Wear a well-tailored pant that falls straight from the hips to the ankles. Pants should always leave room for breathing. If they are too tight, you will look heavier. The wider the pant, the softer the fabric and the wider the pant leg, the longer the length. If you are a long legged petite, you can wear cuffed pants.

Dresses look great on petites. They create an illusion of height. Keep in mind that dresses with slits lengthen legs. Wear soft fabrics and loose knits.

Jacket length is important to the petite woman. When wearing a jacket over a shirt or dress, the length should be kept short in proportion to your body length. Avoid bulky fabrics. Soft, unlined materials are best, because they are thin and flexible.

Skirts can create an illusion of height. A skirt should always look more long than wide. If you are short waisted, keep your waistbands narrow. Wear diagonal pockets and be sure they lay flat.

Petite women should follor the same figure type rules as the average figure types.

full figure women

Approximately 25 million women in the United States wear a size 16 or larger. The body types for women with full figures are straight, full and broad.

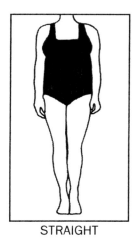
STRAIGHT

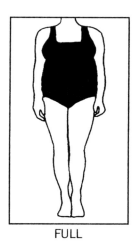
FULL

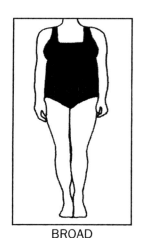
BROAD

GUIDELINES FOR FULL FIGURES

- SHORT NECK: wear loose cowls, V-necks, scoop openings.

- LONG NECK: wear turtlenecks, ascots, and collars.

- HEAVY ARMS: wear tailored 3/4-length sleeves.

- THIN ARMS: wear dolman, raglan, puffy and batwing sleeves.

- THIN LEGS: wear tapered pants.

In choosing a dress for this figure type, choose a lightweight fabric that drapes softly. Shoulder pads, if wide, will balance if you have a triangular figure. Note: you can be both petite and large sized. Many women are.

• Under 5'5": buy 1/2 sizes as they are cut with a high waist and bust. They start at size 12-1/2 and go up from there.

• Over 5'5": buy large sizes as they have lower waistlines and longer hems.

If you are different sizes on the bottom and top, opt for separates. There are many companies that sell clothes as separates and you get an extra advantage—more pieces that work well together!

DO'S & DON'TS FOR FULL FIGURES

DO WEAR:
• Hemlines 3-1/2 inches below your knees
• Elongated objects such as long chains
• Coat dresses
• High boots that meet your hemline
• Natural fibers
• V-neck, scooped and square neck blouses
• Tailored suits
• Draped fabrics
• Oblong scarves
• Bold jewelry
• Loose belts
• Large-brimmed hats

DON'T WEAR:
• Bulky pockets
• Anything too tight
• Anything too short
• Bright colors
• Large plaids
• Flower prints
• Skinny belts.

Remember, what is important is fit. Wear loose-fitting, body-flattering styles.

the little black dress

Although not the originator of the "little black dress" Coco Chanel told Harper's Bazaar in 1923, "Simplicity is the keynote of all true elegance." This was three years before she came out with her first "little black dress." Jean Patou, former lead designer for The House of Patou in Paris was actually the originator and introduced Jersey knits, knee-length hemlines, and trademark use of his shears.

The "little black dress" has become the one fashion piece no woman should be without. "There's nothing to compare it within the modern wardrobe," says Pantaza, who lives in San Francisco. "In one piece you can go from morning errands all the way through late night cocktail parties looking appropriate and chic."

With today's casual dress codes, the sheath is even appropriate for black tie functions and weddings, where black is acceptable today. Black dresses should be loose-fitting to allow the wearer to move freely. What you choose to do with the black dress will depend on your personality.

Durand Guion, Macy's West Fashion Director for Women's Ready to Wear says, "It's simple and sexy and one of the few items that will never let a woman down."

The "little black dress" is a staple and can be accessorized with the changing fashions. Wear with sling back shoes, feminine bags and classic jewelry. Throw a shawl around your neck, add a scarf or cardigan, put on a stylish hat, pearls or wear opaque tights. If you want to expand on black, purchase dresses in chiffon or silk.

Go ahead. Invest in that "little black dress." Purchase the simplest you can find in the highest quality wool fabric. Be sure you choose a dress appropriate to your body type (see examples on following page).

HEAVY ARMS

- elbow-length sleeves conceal heavier arms.

NO WAIST

- wrap dress and tie sash gives a more defined waistline.

SMALL BUST

- empire waist flatters a small bustline.

HEAVY THIGHS

- A-line skirt hides fullest part of thighs and wide neckline helps to balance figure.

shorts

SHORT LEGS

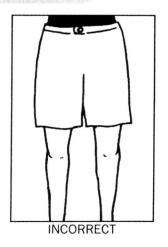

INCORRECT

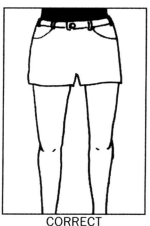

CORRECT
- shorter length makes legs look longer

HEAVY LEGS

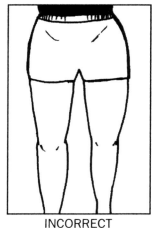

INCORRECT
- tight does not slim!

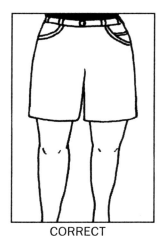

CORRECT
- longer length covers fullest part of legs

FIT GUIDELINES FOR SHORTS

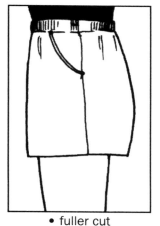

- fuller cut
- elastic does not pull

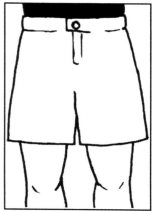

- covers tops of thighs
- looser cut

- woven, tailored waistband

- knit, elastic waist

bathing suit "cover-ups"

LARGE BUST

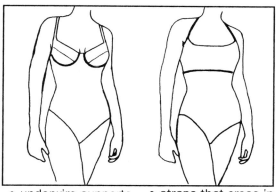

- underwire supports a large bust.
- straps that cross in back add support.

BOTTOM HEAVY

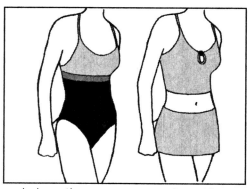

- dark on the bottom to minimize
- a-line skirt minimizes, while top detail draws attention away from bottom

HEAVY OUTER THIGHS

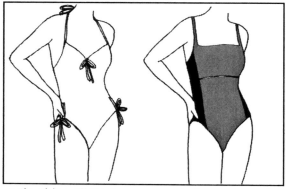

- tie sides allow you to raise and lower legs to flatter

- dark panels make thighs appear slimmer and smoother.

TUMMY BULGE

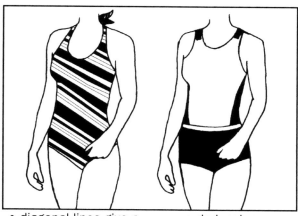

- diagonal lines give a slimming effect

- dark color on stomach and sides minimizes

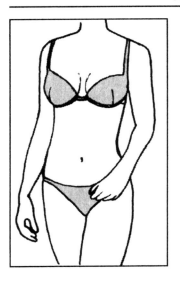

• underwire cups
and outside straps
create cleavage

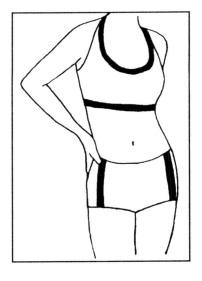

• athletic top
supports bust

• shorts
de-emphasize
buttocks

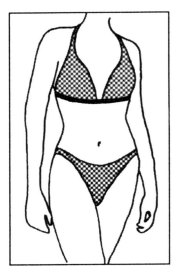

• halter enhances
a small bust

• high leg lengthens
shorter legs

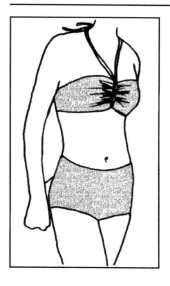

• gathered top shapes a small bust

• boy-short bottoms cover stomach and buttocks

• ruffled gives illusion of more to small bust and boyish hips

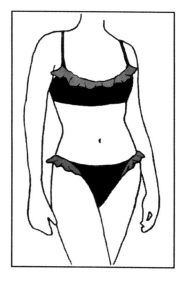

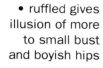

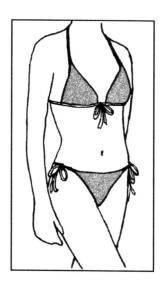

• adjustable flatters fuller hips

Fashion is finding something you're comfortable in and wearing it into the ground.

— Tuesday Weld

coats

GUIDELINES FOR CHOOSING A COAT

We top off our outfit with our outer covering. Coats are worn for warmth, but also for fashion and there are many styles to choose from.

Following are some different types of coats. See if you can pick out which style is best for you.

When choosing a coat, it is best to keep these guidelines in mind:

• COMFORT
Your coat must be comfortable and easy to wear.

• STYLE
Your coat should be the right style for you in proportion. Since a coat is usually worn for more than one season, it has to be able to work well with a lot of your fashion choices. Keep colors and styles in mind. A coat should always cover the longest hem of your dress. Your coat should be flattering. A petite person will not want to choose a large bulky tent coat with large shoulder pads. If you are heavy, avoid a bulky, heavy fabric, whereas a thin person looks great in this type of coat.

• FABRIC
Choose a fabric that will wear well such as wool or cashmere. These fabrics last a long time.

• FIT
Be sure that the coat you choose is roomy enough for heavy sweaters. The arms should be comfortable and not too tight.

TYPES OF COATS

REEFER

Has narrow lapels
and is long and lean,
usually with side
seam pockets.

WRAP

Soft casual look for
over jeans, worn
over another coat
for warmth; many
different uses.

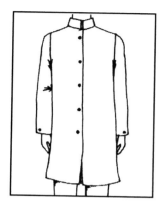

MANDARIN

A standup collar adds height for a feminine, polished look.

TRENCH

Double breasted with epaulets, belt and storm flaps; very versatile, can be worn day or evening; adapts to various climates.

STADIUM

Sporty coat, double breasted with toggle buttons; wool or cotton with plaid lining and a hood.

CAPE

Unconstructed, sleeveless, full wrap worn over another coat; looks especially good on taller people; should not cling; attractive when combined with boots.

SWEATER

A type of coat for between seasons in a lighter weight knitted material.

REDINGOTE

Double breasted with a defined waist; attractive on all body types.

BALMACAAN

Loose fitting raglan sleeved coat with small collar and button front.

CHESTERFIELD

Single breasted, distinguished classic style usually with velvet or fur collar; accentuates a youthful look.

Fashionable women don't just put on fashionable clothes... the truly fashionable are beyond fashion.

– Ceal Beaton

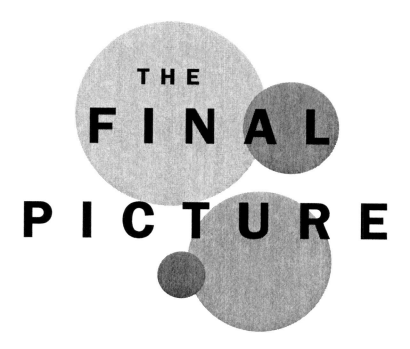

accessories

Nothing enhances the total look of an outfit like the perfect necklace, pin, scarf, shoes, or hose. Accessories add color, pattern, texture, and interest to an outfit—the finishing touch that defines your look. Through the use of accessories, ordinary clothing can come alive and make a personal statement. Have fun with your clothes and become a trend setter.

JEWELRY

Keep size and proportion in mind. Petites require smaller accessories than larger women.

- Drop earrings lengthen.
- Keep jewelry lightweight in milder weather.
- Bolder jewelry should be limited to a few pieces.
- Bracelets shorten long arms and call attention to attractive hands.

BELTS

Narrow belts enhance short waisted women. Worn slightly below the natural waistline, they create better proportion.

HOSIERY

- To make legs appear longer, wear shorter skirts with tinted or opaque hose that match your skirt color.
- Patterned hose are complementary for thin legs.
- Wear your sheerest stockings with your dressier shoe styles.

GLOVES

Gloves should be lighter or a similar color to the sleeve you have on. Generally speaking, a short glove is appropriate for daytime, longer for evening dress.

SHOES

The right footwear completes your outfit. Choose shoes that are matched to your stockings and this will elongate your leg. For thin legs, choose thin and lightweight shoes to add bulk.

The weight and style of a shoe depend on the dressiness of the outfit and the weight of the fabric of which it is made. The longer the skirt, the lighter weight the shoe. Heel height can vary with fashion trends.

Lightweight fabrics need a lightweight shoe whereas skirts in sportier fabrics like wool, plaids and tweeds can be worn with heavier shoes and look great with textured or opaque stockings.

Shoes with heavier soles look good with heavy socks.

Flat shoes may be worn with long, sweeping skirts. Culottes and longer skirts look great with boots. A V-vamp on the shoe will lengthen your leg. Rounder toes make legs appear shorter. Choose pointy toes in order to add visual length.

Slacks that narrow at the ankle need a lighter weight shoe. The dressiness of the slacks and the material they are made of have a lot to do with what shoe style and material are most appropriate.

A dressier slack style, make of a heavier fabric like wool, looks better when combined with a casual shoe. More delicate fabrics need lighter weight shoes no matter what the slack style. Dressier slacks require dressier shoe styles.

Large women should match their hose to their shoe color. Your hemline should meet the top of your boot. Avoid wearing ankle or T-strap shoes on larger legs.

HANDBAGS

Handbags come in all shapes and sizes, but there are only a few colors and shapes that are adaptable to any type of look. A black, cream, or white handbag in an envelope style will take you anywhere!

If your shoulder strap is too long, tie it or take it to a shoemaker for repair. Large breasted women should opt for low-slung purse, away from the bust.

Purses do not have to match your shoes but it is wise to stay in the same color family.

Large women can carry larger purses appropriately in proportion to their size. Petite women should stick to smaller handbags that will not overpower their appearance.

A word about briefcases—either you carry a handbag or you carry a briefcase. If you must use both, put your handbag inside your briefcase.

SCARVES

Scarves can indeed make an outfit special and can easily be transformed into mufflers, bows, ascots, ties, belts, and even jackets. They come in all shapes and sizes: big squares, little squares, oblongs, and bias folds.

• Long silk scarves tied around the neck and knotted below the chest pull the eye away from an area you want to minimize.
• An oblong scarf can be substituted for a belt. This scarf is versatile since it can be worn at the waist, neck or even around the crown of a hat.
• Scarves made of lightweight fabrics are good since they can drape and/or be pleated easily and knotted with little extra bulk.
• Draping a scarf over one shoulder will emphasize a necessary vertical line.
• Drape a scarf at the neck in place of a necklace to form a V-neck.

SCARF STYLES

To acheive Bow and Puff styles, use an oblong scarf.

A BOW: to make a Bow, slip scarf around your neck, leaving the left side longer than the right side. Wrap the left side around the right and pull the left end through the loop.

A PUFF: to make a Puff, double the scarf, making one end longer and loop it over the shorter end. Pull the longer end to where it looks most attractive.

 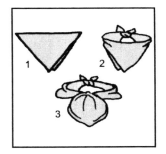

A SQUARE: using a square scarf, fold into a triangle, placing the pointed end in front and knotting the ends in back. Also use a square as a handkerchief. Works under jackets in lieu of a blouse. Fold scarf in triangle, place point in front, cross ends in back, then bring forward and knot.

AN ASCOT: to achieve an Ascot look, use an oblong scarf.

A SQUARE KNOT: to make a square knot, cross one end of the scarf over the other and loop. Cross opposite end over and knot

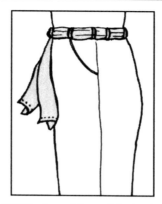

A CUMBERBUND OR BELT: to achieve this look, use an oblong scarf. It
works best when using a scarf cut on the bias.

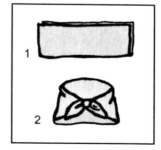

A SOFT DRAPE: to make a soft drape, take an oblong scarf and tie a small
knot at the end of the scarf. Bring around the neck and pull through.

A JABOT: to make a Jabot, fold scarf horizontally to form an oblong. Flip ends over one another.

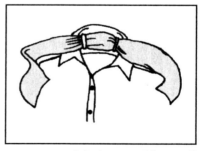

FABRIC LOOP: these are sewn right into necklines of blouses. Take two inches of square fabric into double thickness (you can use the fabric from a hem or inside facing). Bring stitched ends up and over the neckline and pin from inside. You can make this from velvet, taffeta, satin, leather, suede or felt. Add versatility to prints by adding solid loops. Sew two different color bows together and thread through loop.

hemlines

With hemlines moving up, the right length becomes a fashion issue for women. How short is not as important as selecting the right length for each style and for your individual figure type.

HOURGLASS figure types can wear many lengths because they are in proportion.

STRAIGHT figure types should modify their skirt lengths with an eye toward basic proportions—the slimmer your shape, the shorter your skirts can be.

TRIANGULAR figure types should wear skirts around the knee or below, balanced with jacket styles that do not cut the body at the widest point.

INVERTED TRIANGLE figure types can wear lengths to the extreme—from very short and flared to long and flowing.

GUIDELINES FOR SKIRT AND DRESS LENGTHS

• CLASSIC SKIRT should be about 1-1/2" to 3" below knee cap with shoe weight being light to medium.

• SHORT SKIRT should fall below knee cap and up, with light to medium shoe.

• MID-CALF SKIRT should be about 3" to 4" below the knee to about 3" above ankle bone with light to medium shoe.

• ANKLE LENGTH SKIRT should be about 2" above ankle bone to just below ankle bone with a light weight shoe.

• FLOOR LENGTH SKIRT or dress should just cover the foot to the floor with a light to medium weight shoe.

PANT LENGTHS

Pant lengths can be confusing. In determining length, long means almost to the floor (1/2-1") in the back with your shoe on. The types of pants that would require this length would be a straight wide leg, straight classic leg (9" across), and flared leg. Semi-long means covering the foot with the shoe on and covering part of the heel on the shoe approximately 2" from the floor. The type of pant that would require this length would be the straight classic leg. Both long and semi-long are similar—short covers ankle bone as in tapered and harem pants.

In determining shoe weight, light resembles a low, tiny strap sandal; wedgies and platforms are considered heavy weight.

The shorter the pant, the lighter weight the shoe should be. The lighter and more delicate the fabric of the slack, the lighter weight the shoe should be.

The narrower the slack at the ankle, the lighter weight the shoe should be. The dressiness of the pant and the material it is made of determines what shoe style and material is most appropriate.

Very sporty shoes are only right with more casual fabrics, but a slightly dressier shoe will go with both casual and dressier fabrics.

More delicate fabrics need lighter weight shoes no matter what style of pants.

Dressy pants require dressy shoe styles.

foot notes

FEET TALK

Your feet carry most of your weight. Just as you take care of your hands, you should care for your feet. Use a pumice stone to remove dead skin. At night, use a rich cream or vaseline to soften feet. Witch hazel works well after baths. Baking soda added to a foot bath relieves dry skin. Give yourself a pedicure after a bath or shower, or after soaking. Cut your nails straight across, file, push cuticles back, put cotton balls between toes to separate. Put on two clear base coats, and polish in a color like your nail color. Add top coat.

ENHANCING LARGE FEET

• It is best to stay in a monochromatic look. A darker hose similar to the color of the shoe accomplishes this.

• Rounded or squared-off shoes will give the appearance of a thinner foot.

• Ankle strap shoes accentuate width and length of your foot.

• High heels always make legs look more attractive.

• A basic pump is the best choice in style due to the small amount of shoe that is shown on the foot. If you want to break up the length of your feet, try open-toed or cut-out shoes.

• Wear boots, especially with a lot of detail, in a mid-size heel.

ENHANCING SMALL FEET

- You can wear ankle straps and anklets.

- Wear textured hose and shoes.

- Ankle high boots are flattering on you.

- Look for detail on the shoes.

- Wear high-top shoes.

- Keep your clothing in proportion to the shoes you wear.

I firmly believe that what gives other people a sense of what and who they are in is the way they are dressed. It is the first impression. I can't think of a man, who, whether in business or leisure, does not want to project authority.

– Bill Blass

YOUR PROFESSIONAL IMAGE

Anything the mind can conceive, and believe, it can accomplish
– David Sarnoff

personal image

Many people believe that personal image is just about wearing the right clothes. Clothing is an essential part of nonverbal communication but not the only component. Many other factors are important to consider in order to achieve "polish" in your image. Paying attention to what is appropriate within your organization is crucial. Inappropriate clothing can send negative messages of indifference or disregard for others.

NONVERBAL COMMUNICATION

One of the ways we create our professional image is through nonverbal communication. This includes movement of a part of the body, such as a nod of the head or raising of the eyebrows or movement of the entire body, such as overall body tension or jumping up and down. It is not always easy to perceive various meanings of body language because this involves interpretation. If someone appears to you like they are upset, you may be interpreting that they are in a bad mood, while in reality, this look may be totally unintentional and that person may not be aware they look this way.

The study of body motion or kinesics involves the study of body movements in communication. It is estimated that the verbal part of some conversation accounts for less than 35% of social meaning of the conversation. Sixty-five percent is carried by non-speaking messages. This is what makes the understanding of nonverbal language so important. Body movement and positions can be considered either reflexive (involuntary) or non-reflexive. One reflexive indication is pupil dilation. At a Kinesics Convention, Dr. Edward H. Hess explained that clinical studies have shown that the pupil unconsciously widens when the eye sees something pleasant or exciting. Non-reflexive body language can be much more difficult to interpret. Many times, people can fake gestures. Look at a picture of yourself when you were genuinely happy and compare it to a posed picture. It is nearly impossible to hide how we are feeling. We believe in political leaders, actors, trial lawyers, and salespeople when they believe in themselves and this will come through in their body language.

PRACTICE THESE GUIDELINES... MAKE THEM HABITS!

• People who speak in a louder voice and those who speak more slowly are perceived to be more powerful and believable.

• The fewer hand and body gestures you make, the more powerful and intelligent you will appear to be.

• Leaders and powerful people take up more space than other people. They tend to lean slightly forward with their arms and legs relaxed and slightly spread. By taking up more space, they appear to be taking charge.

• The person that has a high eye level is usually perceived as the leader. People tend to address that person first.

• Smiling makes a person seem friendly and more attractive.

• There are no gender differences with handshakes. Shake hands with confidence.

• Become aware of your energy and other people's energy.

• Stand casually with good posture and keep in good body alignment.

Most nonverbal messages of dress are unintentionally communicated and unintentionally received. For example, if you are dressed in jeans and a tee-shirt, other people may unconsciously think you are not a professional person or that you have a low academic background.

Knowing and understanding the effect clothing has on people will give you power and will reduce the number of messages that are unintentionally sent and received. In order to have effective communication, both the sender and the receiver need to be consciously aware of what messages are being sent.

Clothing is a language. The wearer gives a message which is transmitted by clothing through a visual channel which is decoded by another person. The perceptions of the person receiving the information or the person who is observing it is what matters. McGraw discovered that the self-esteem of the wearer is involved in this decision:

"When you know who you are, then you know how you look. All these little extras just fall into place. You learn about your body. When people present themselves physically, you can tell how they feel about themselves."

Dress codes in business are based on the assumption that the perceptions of the public are most important. The research findings indicate that perceptions are made and in most cases represent stereotypes about clothing, A police officer gets compliance from citizens because of his uniform. A nun demands respect and compliance due to her habit. Dress does have an effect on people. Graduates wear clothing that signifies achievement. People respond to clothing messages. Some of the things clothing "communicates" are whether you are powerful or not powerful, credible or non-credible, trustworthy or not trustworthy, aggressive or passive, or likeable or not likeable. People can determine by looking at your clothing things like your economic status, social status, and degree of professionalism. Most of all, what you choose to wear tells people how you feel about yourself. Clothing also affects your behavior. If you wear something you like, you will get a psychological lift and perform better.

It is not by accident that people are powerful. They submit to the paradigm, "If you fail to plan, you plan to fail." They know what they want, and they learn the steps necessary to reach their goal. They tend to be organized. As a behavior and values counselor, I've observed hundreds of powerful people and found that these people were dominant and individualistic in nature and knew exactly what they were doing and where they were going. These people, while appearing to be somewhat relaxed, were very uptight. They have a goal and they will do whatever they have to get to the goal. They will dress the part, act the part, be the part. They will emulate successful people. They will learn from successful people. They will learn to talk like successful people. They learn the power position, such as standing with perfect posture and poise, standing erect and spreading their feet slightly. They hire professionals and mentors to inform them on how to be their best.

To accomplish the "look" of a power person, it is necessary to be "an expert on yourself." A full-length mirror to see yourself as others see you, and an audio tape player to hear yourself as others hear you are good first steps. If you have video tapes you have been in, these can be helpful tools for evaluating how you look to others. The goal is to determine your sense of presence.

The power look has always consisted of the traditional suit, white shirt and fine accessories. Finding your individual style is discovering your uniqueness. To project a powerful image requires that you package yourself appropriate to your profession. Although diet and exercise can help to reshape your body, you are who you are through genetics. Some people are short, some tall, some thin, and some stocky. If your shoulders are broad and thin, if your arms are short or long, this is not going to change! Your silhouette is what is important in determining your body type. A silhouette describes the basic cut and shape of a garment and this needs to be your main consideration when purchasing clothing.

Personal grooming is just as important as what you wear. Improper grooming will ruin any image you work to project.

COMPONENT	GROOMING
Hair	Clean, trimmed and neatly arranged.
Nails	Neat, clean and trimmed
Teeth	Brushed, no gaps.
Breath	Tobacco, alcohol and coffee have odors, avoid these
Body	Bathed, showered—use deodorant
Perfumes	Use sparingly, or not at all

psychology of color

When you see lights flashing, a siren blasting, or a red fire truck, you react. Color does affect the emotions and symbolizes many things for people. People choose their clothing and accessories according to their taste in color. Color surrounds us. Technology makes it possible to choose from so many colors and prints. At one time, the color purple was available only to royalty because of the exclusiveness of the dye. People respond strongly to color.

The three primary colors are red, yellow, and blue. These three colors plus black and white form all other colors. Primaries and combinations of two primaries create color families (hues), which bring about reds, oranges, yellows, greens, blues, and purples. All colors involve temperature (warm or cool undertones), depth (lightness or darkness), and intensity (brightness) or quiet nature of a color.

Psychologists say that color means different things to different people. It is believed that color aesthetics are learned and that they are somewhat cultural. Color can stimulate, excite, depress, soothe, and affect your state of mind. Psychologists have demonstrated in laboratories that warm colors such as orange-red, yellow, and orange can raise blood temperature and stimulate appetite. Red can step up your heartbeat, and blue can slow it down. Think of "seeing red" when you are upset and "feeling blue" when you are down.

It would be a good idea to have a professional work with you to see what colors will bring out your best.

Ladies Dress Guide

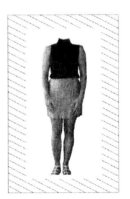

Casual	■		▨	Formal
Daily	▦		▨	Social
Power	▨		▨	Inappropriate

official dress guide

It is recognizable that dress and image are important. Standards for dress codes are already in place of hundreds of occupations. Businesses recognize that dress and image have an effect on people. This effect can be negative or positive. A dress code establishes a sense of unity among employees within an occupation. Although dress codes may set a limit on personal choice, conforming to an established dress code offers the advantage of working in a team environment within a larger organization that symbolizes the importance of the company. Customer research has found that certain clothing choices denote professionalism, dedication, and pride for the company for which one works. The old adage, "You don't get a second chance to make a good first impression" is still true. In and out of the workplace, you will be judged by your clothing communication.

The basic business suit is still the acceptable norm for both the power and daily business attire. Even though business casual has been implemented in many places of business, when you have a client meeting scheduled, the client comes first. They need to feel comfortable with you. When meeting with clients out of the office, regular business attire is what is appropriate (suit, scarf), unless the company you represent has in place a business casual policy and you are invited to participate in their policy. For meetings in the office, your dress should be appropriate to your clients' expectations. Keep in mind that without clients there is no business. The clothing you choose to wear can and will have an effect on your customer.

SIX CATEGORIES OF DRESS

The following categories will help you to "package" yourself for your particular occupation. Different careers have different wardrobe needs. In banking and accounting, this may be a classic suit. In retail, education, and sales, suits or blazers can work, and in construction, jeans are suitable. In the field of entertainment, art, fashion, and interior design, an unconstructed suit may be warranted.

POWER DRESS

Your suit needs to fit as it were made for your body. A power suit is always custom-made. This suit is intended to make a strong visual impact on your business image. If you choose to wear a double-breasted suit, the buttons must stay buttoned and should match the color of the suit.

Unless there is a business casual policy in place, professional businesses that are traditional such as banks, insurance companies, accounting firms, and stockbrokers normally wear two-piece single-breasted wool suit in a medium weight fabric. A crisp white or cream long-sleeved blouse, or scarf, will tie in with a background color and quality leather accessories.

DAILY DRESS

If you want a job, you have to look the part. Dressing successfully will enable you to get that promotion, earn that respect, and move up the corporate ladder. The most important wardrobe item is the business suit. Buy the best you can afford. Wool or wool blends are a must in a business wardrobe.

The traditional colors for a suit for women are black, brown, gray, winter white, taupe, hunter green, navy blue, turquoise, and medium blues.

Blouses for women are white/cream, fuchsia, purple, pink, and turquoise, and are in silk, rayon, and cotton fabrics.

The best scarf colors for traditional business wear are red, dark blue, teal, purple, olive, and taupe. Traditional dressing requires fine accessories, such as leather belts, linen handkerchiefs, gold watch and jewelry, and leather shoes and handbag.

Businesses that involve manual labor and office activity, such as engineering, manufacturing, or transportation allow for a more relaxed daily dress requirement.

You should always dress business-like and avoid extremes in your personal appearance. Shirts should have a collar, and skirts, pants, culottes, dress, and flat shoes are appropriate.

Creative environments such as retail, decorating, cosmetic companies, and publishing may require a wool two-piece suit and pearls for women.

CASUAL DRESS

The casual trend began in 1990 in Canada when many companies introduced a dress-down day as part of their annual Fall United Way Campaign.

- *About 15 million of the 118 million employees in American work-places dress casually at work.*
- *About 90% of Americans wear casual clothes to work at least some of the time.*
- *Fifty-three percent of white-collar workers are allowed to dress casually every day, a 20% increase from 1995. And 90% of all US Business has a casual business wear policy.*

– Levi Strauss and Company

One of the reasons market researchers say that companies have moved toward casual business wear is due to baby-boomers, who grew up in jeans and never wanted to wear the gray flannel suit. What you wear to work influences how people will treat you. What you wear will affect your professionalism and how people will perceive you. Since you have to go to work anyway and you have the option of appearing professional and competent, isn't it better to look professional and either stay in your current position or move up the corporate ladder? Most of the time, even with casual days in effect in many of our corporations, we believe, and research shows, that most of the time you should still wear traditional clothing meant for work. If you look at successful men and women, you will notice they choose dark, solid colors for their wardrobes and always wear suits.

In today's competitive workplace, whether it is technological, service, or retail, it is now more important than ever to dress appropriately for your job. Casual dress was created to take the image of rigid gray flannel suits to a more creative and entrepreneurial dress with the purpose of combining power suit authority with comfort. The gray flannel suit of the 1950's imposed conformity thought necessary at the time in corporations. Today's corporations are changing. There is downsizing, mergers, acquisitions, and change in management on a regular basis. There are many jobs available, and people are thinking about changing to a company that can offer them what they are looking for. There are young people in their twenties who are working from their homes and producing Fortune 500 companies. For these people, clothing is not an issue. However, when they go out to represent their service or product to a client, they will need to know about the appropriate dress code to succeed. Casual dress is about comfort, neatness, and professionalism.

What is right for casual days for a computer guru is just not right for an accountant's office. It may be that a blazer or casual pantsuit are as casual as your company may want.

Your clothes must work with your market, your environment, your clients, and your colleagues. By knowing how your business associates dress and observing how you expect the people they meet to dress is critical. It is okay to ask them what they deem appropriate for your particular business.

It is important to make others feel comfortable. You need to know where you are going and how to practice business etiquette, which is to observe clothing customs. You must fit into your client's culture. If you have a relaxed dress code in your office, keep a blazer and dress blouse and appropriate shoe in your office. You never know when the senior vice-president will decide to see how your department is doing.

Recruiters assume how you look at your interview will be the most professional you will ever look.

APPROPRIATE BUSINESS CASUAL

- Blazer or sweater set
- Basic skirts/prints
- Two-piece dresses in soft fabrics
- Small textured socks
- Tights, pants, or hosiery
- Cotton shirts
- Coordinated clothing

INAPPROPRIATE BUSINESS CASUAL

- T-shirts of any kind
- Jeans of any kind
- Sandals
- Shorts
- Revealing clothing or low-cut shirts
- Sun dresses
- Worn, torn or stained clothing
- Weekend clothing
- Open-toe shoes
- Strappy or slip-on shoes
- No socks

SOCIAL DRESS

It is very different when you choose social dress for a work environment. When dressing socially, it is not imperative that you wear a suit and you can choose a comfortable shoe, however, you should ALWAYS have fine fabrics and look your best. A social occasion gives you the opportunity to show your individuality.

FORMAL DRESS

Formal dress is the ultimate in dressing. This is the time for long gowns for women and tuxedos for men.

BUSINESS GUIDELINES FOR WOMEN

	POWER	DAILY	SOCIAL	CASUAL	INAPPROPRIATE
JACKETS	fitted jacket solid neutrals wool fabrics	blazer vest	blazer sweater	details/trim printed fabrics	anything tight or clingy
SKIRTS/ PANTS	fitted	tailored shirt dress pants	basic colors casual materials	printed fabrics	too open slits
BLOUSES	collared solids cottons	circle necks square necks	turtlenecks elbow sleeves soft prints	printed fabrics sleeveless tops (worn w/ jacket)	cleavage
DRESSES	tailored (to knee) coat dress quality fabric	tailored wool or silk	2-piece dress prints or soft fabrics pant suits	cotton knits prints	above the knee anything too open/clingy
ACCESSORIES	leather hosiery (in nude or tan)	leather hosiery (in nude or tan)	straw or textured tote tights	trim belts high heels black hosiery	toes exposed platforms or slides no hosiery

WOMEN'S WARDROBE

- Two suits - one solid - one muted - must coordinate

- Two Jackets - one solid, one muted

- Three Skirts - to go with jackets

- Four Blouses - neutral, accent, white, cream, solid -all long sleeve

- Two Sweaters

- One two-piece suit (solid)

- One Long Coat

- Three Shoes - neutral - closed toe pump or baby doll style

- One Purse - solid (either carry a purse of a briefcase -not both)

- 2-3 scarves or necklaces (gold, silver) or pins

- 2 Belts -leather and worn loosely

- 12 pair of nylons in neutral shades-pant socks should be plain or very lightly patterned

REMEMBER TO USE THE "COST-PER-WEAR" FORMULA!

The true cost of anything that you buy is not the amount you actually paid. It is the number of times you ultimately wear it. Therefore, an expensive garment may be a lifetime investment if you wear it often.

EXAMPLES:

1 business suit bought for $300
worn 25 times
costs $12 each wear

1 evening dress bought for $250
worn 4 times
costs $62.50 each wear

YOUR SOUL

Self respect cannot be hunted. It cannot be purchased. It is never for sale. It comes to us when we are alone, in quiet moments, in quiet places, when we suddenly realize that knowing the good, we have done it, knowing the beautiful, we have served it, knowing the truth, we have spoken it.

— Whitney Griswold

When we think of Image, what comes to mind is our outer appearance—how we appear to others. But, what about the "inside?" Is it really true that "It's not what's on the outside that counts?" While it is true that we are judged in a very short period of time on our outer appearance, and that accounts for much of an impression that is made, there needs to be a balance between what we appear to be on the outside and what we actually are on the inside.

Beauty today has a new definition. In the 1800's beauty meant something to be looked at, admired, copied, or painted. These are superficial qualities. Beauty today has an inward feeling—a total experience for both men and women emotionally, psychologically, and aesthetically. It is actually being in control and being challenged. If you feel beautiful you will feel confident, relaxed, and ready for anything that requires your performance. Beauty should not lie in the eyes of the beholder, but in the heart of the possessor. In the story of The Ugly Duckling by Hans Christian Anderson, when the duckling had been convinced by everyone that he was ugly, nothing seemed to go right. But, when he saw a true reflection of himself he rejoiced from his heart, "I never dreamed of so much happiness when I was the ugly duckling." Beauty brings confidence and confidence is the magic behind what it takes to be successful in both your personal and/or professional life.

Do you see yourself as a "victim?" Do you blame people for what happens in your life? Are you positive towards other people or do you have negative feelings toward them? Only when you understand the answers to these questions will you be able to succeed in life and become a person who is whole from Head to Soul.

The next time you have trouble falling or staying asleep or you cannot concentrate on something someone is saying, think about the conversa-tion you are having within yourself and try to make yourself aware of your inner voice. Who is talking within you? Do you have feelings that you have not worked through? Talk out loud and discover how to remedy this situation. Perhaps you are thinking about an upcoming assignment at work and it is keeping you up at night or someone in your family said something to you and you just cannot get it out of your mind. Dr. Frederick Perls, a Freudian analyst, used this principle to invent Gestalt Therapy.

Gestalt is a German word that means an organized whole. He perceived that many personalities lack wholeness and have fragmented personalities. He felt people are often aware of only parts of themselves instead of their whole self. The purpose of this type of therapy was to help people to become whole and to help them to become aware of, admit to, reclaim, and bring together their fragmented parts. A person needs, he felt, to be self-sufficient and have an inner support system within their soul and not need to receive this from any other source.

There are many people who feel they need another person to be whole. We have all heard in introductions, "This is my other half," or "This is my better half." If we are to develop on the inside, then it is very important that we are self-reliant. This interprets into not having the need to depend on a significant other, job title, academic achievement, or bank balance to feel whole in your soul. Your capabilities of what you can do and who you are should be internal in the knowledge that you can depend always on you.

Perl suggests you use the word "I" instead of the word "it" in order to assume responsibility for your behaviors. He developed what is known today as the "chair technique" whereby you have two chairs opposite one another and you sit in one chair and communicate your thoughts and then sit in the other chair and communicate back to yourself. This "hot seat" method was used with a teacher in his study who thought of herself as friendly but did not understand why she did not have any close friends. She empathically denied any angry feelings, though others described her as an angry person. When the teacher roleplayed her fragmented self, she acted her friendly self from the hot seat and imagined her angry self on the opposite chair. The dialogue went something like this:

"I don't know why I'm here. I'm always so nice."
"You do know why you are here. You don't have any close friends."
"I don't understand. I'm always trying to help people."
"That's the problem. You're always helpful and people feel obligated to you."

Within a short time, the teacher heard herself getting loud and realized her anger. She was now ready to admit that she could be so angry.

The LikeAbility Profile™

What is your self image?
Do you like yourself?
Take the LikeAbility Profile™ and find out!

1. Are you a friend of yours?

2. Do you greet people with a smile, give your hand, look them in the eye and give your name with pride?

3. When you answer the telephone, do you answer it with a smile and give your name?

4. Do you invest in your own special knowledge?

5. Do you always say "thank you?"

6. Do you accept compliments well?

7. Do you keep your problems to yourself unless they directly relate to the situation?

8. Do you consciously try not to make excuses to people?

9. Can you avoid bragging about yourself?

10. Do you accept you for who you are?

11. Do you enjoy your life?

12. Do you look at unsuccessful experiences as opportunities to learn and change?

13. Do you look at ridicule as ignorance?

14. Do you handle constructive criticism well?

15. Do you enjoy doing things for yourself, without feeling guilty?

16. Can you adapt to stressful situations?

17. When you make comments to yourself, are they of a positive nature?

18. Do you seek out positive and successful, motivated people to associate with and use as role models?

19. Do you want to be involved and contribute something to this world?

20. Do you want to be important?

21. Are you an honest person?

22. Are you a sincere person?

23. Are you a sensitive person?

24. Do you have the best posture for your anatomical structure?

25. Are you open to new ideas and to other peoples' opinions? Are you able to see the "other side?"

26. Do you have a sense of humor?

27. Do you stand up for yourself?

28. Do you have good listening skills?

29. Do you like to learn?

30. Do you like yourself?

Evaluation

• If you answered no to less than 3 or 4 questions, you are exteremely likeable and are very close to being the best person one can be.

• If you answered no to less than 8 questions, you are still likeable, but need to consider turning more negatives into positives.

• If you answered no to more than 8 to 10 questions, you should probably re-evaluate yourself, your life and your goals.

Take this profile periodically to re-evaluate after self improvement is realized.

One of the most important elements of success is self awareness. It is the ability to step back from life and take a good look at who you are and how you relate to your environment. It is the ability to accept yourself as a unique individual and to be able to recognize your potential, as well as your limitations.

Self awareness is being honest in what you see, knowing your strengths and weaknesses, knowing what you can contribute and recognizing that both time and effort will be necessary to achieve this. A winner will be able to look in the mirror and like what they see. A winner tries all through life to be the very best in thought, word, and deed.

This instrument is a self-awareness tool to be used for measuring LikeAbility. If you do not like yourself, you'll have difficulty accepting other peoples' love. Next to psychological, safety and social needs are the need to be someone and to feel that you have something to contribute. This is called self-actualization and according to Maslow is the ultimate need. Socrates says, "Know thyself."

ATrademarked creation fromThe ImageMaker, Inc.
www.imagemaker1.com

Do you know someone who lights up a room when he or she enters? Or a person who seems comfortable with everyone they meet? The type of person who knows how to make others feel comfortable is a person who feels comfortable within. This is someone who has charm.

Charm is a glow within a woman that casts a most becoming light on others.

— *John Mason Brown*

Charm is the ability to be friendly, energetic, kind, and caring whatever the circumstances. It is an attitude toward yourself, toward others, and toward the world in which you live. Charm comes from within. "Smile, and the world smiles with you." A smile gives a silent message that says, "I am approachable, and I like you." People will respond favorably to people they like, and people like people who like them. The person who smiles has made the other person feel comfortable.

CARING
Caring comes from within. It is important to care about yourself but also important to care about others. You receive a strong feeling of self-satisfaction when you care for others. What you give to others will reap an added benefit for you if you ever need someone to care about you.

ETIQUETTE
Etiquette is also an inner quality. You show that you care about yourself by understanding the importance of good manners. It does not cost anything to be pleasant. A person who cares about himself or herself also cares about others. A simple "thank you," "you're welcome," "I'm sorry, I was wrong," or "excuse me" are cleansing words. Writing a thank you note or giving someone a remembrance are simple and thoughtful ways that will provide you with inner serenity and confidence as a human being.

POSTURE & BODY LANGUAGE
Posture and Body Language exhibit inner confidence. Good

posture "says" to others, "I feel good about myself." What we say with our hands, eyes, eyebrows, walk, and facial expressions often speaks louder than any words or sentences we use. Keep in mind that body language is an extremely important tool. Statistics have shown that we are being judged mostly on our outer body appearance. This is known as nonverbal communication. A true understanding of how we appear to others can make it easier to send more effective messages.

WHAT THEY DO	**WHAT THEY "SAY"!**
raised eyebrows	surprise, questioning
shaky hands	uneasy, uncomfortable
tapping feet	nervous, hurried
limp handshake	lack of confidence
lowered chin	shy

It is important to know that what you do may result in others thinking something entirely different from what you intended your message to be!

For you to be the best you can be, you must possess the ingredients for a beautiful inner personality to shine through. What you are on the inside is crucial to making the outside appearance work for you. Have you ever had a friend who was a wonderful person but did not consider outside appearance a priority for them? Or, did you have a friend that looked great all of the time but did not possess those inner qualities? Imagine giving each friend the "balance ingredient" for total success.

Outer Appearance + Inner Qualities = Total Beauty

Yes, it is true that what is on the outside does count but the really important things in life are not found on the outside of our bodies. Qualities such as kindness, caring, and love make people happy and confident. Although we are judged on what people see, and this will "open doors" for you, once you go through that door, you need to continue to make a positive impression—a lasting impression that makes others comfortable being with you.

Image is a total process by which you develop your look on the outside have your own individual style. Then you work to develop your inner self to achieve happiness and self-confidence.You cannot be useful to someone else unless you have identified "who you are." There are instruments that measure behavior and values that do this.

It takes courage and commitment to experience the freedom of being whole, to take a stand on something you believe in, to say to your significant other or a colleague, "I'm sorry you feel that way." It takes courage and belief in yourself to choose being authentic over receiving approval. The saying, "It's lonely at the top" is true if you allow it to be. You must accept responsibility for your own choices, and as long as you feel in your heart that you do the "right thing," you will have the courage to not allow yourself to be influenced by outside forces.

Consider the following "keys for success:"

• Look at where you are now. Where would you like to be?

• What will it take to reach your goal?

• Remember that you create you own success. Rid yourself of any negative thoughts.

• What type of roadblocks are keeping you from the success that you deserve?

If you have the courage, you will reach self-actualization and experience a feeling only a self-actualized person can feel. It is a feeling of wholeness from the inside out—From Head to Soul. Image is a total process by which you develop your look on the outside and have your own individual style. Then you work to develop your inner self to achieve happiness and self-confidence. A person who has mastered the art of total image is a person who has inner and outer qualities. It is a person who is beautiful from the inside out.

Set the course of your life by the three stars - sincerity, courage and unselfishness. From these flow a host of other virtues...He who follows them will obtain the highest type of success: that which lies in the esteem of others.

— Dr. Monroe E. Deutch

Success breeds success...and more success and more success!

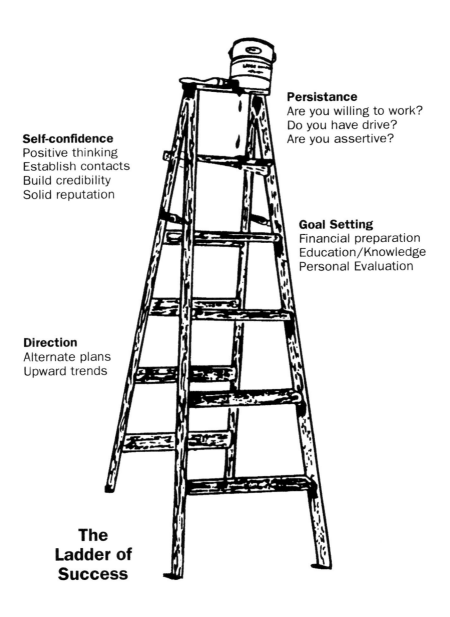

Persistance
Are you willing to work?
Do you have drive?
Are you assertive?

Self-confidence
Positive thinking
Establish contacts
Build credibility
Solid reputation

Goal Setting
Financial preparation
Education/Knowledge
Personal Evaluation

Direction
Alternate plans
Upward trends

The Ladder of Success